101
WAYS TO GET
OVER YOUR
EX-GIRLFRIEND

First published in Great Britain in 2005 by Unstuck Books, an imprint of Orana Publishing Limited

www.unstuckbooks.com

A CIP catalogue record for this book is available from the British Library.

ISBN 0955075114

Cover design and typesetting: Reluctant Hero
www.reluctanthero.com

Printed and bound in the United Kingdom by Century 23, Edinburgh.

101
WAYS TO GET
OVER YOUR
EX-GIRLFRIEND

written by
Shaun Baines and Graham Rickman

INTRODUCTION

As the great ABBA once proclaimed - "Breaking up is never easy, I know." Well, we know. We know all too well. We've been dumped by every demographic of woman going. Except maybe by women who are well adjusted, happy and beautiful, but that's only because you've got a better chance of finding Bigfoot than one of them.

Throughout the years, we've been given the brush off, given the boot, been let go and cut loose. We've been told "I prefer you as a friend," "I look upon you as a brother" and "You've let yourself go." In short, we've been dropped like a three hundred pound ballerina so many times we've learned to expect the worst. This is what makes us uniquely qualified to give you advice on getting through these dark days ahead.

Contrary to popular belief, we're not a couple of losers. In fact, we're nice, educated young men, if a little bitter. Well, frighteningly bitter, actually. Like the majority of men, however, we're not great with women. We've tried the flowers and poetry technique and we've tried to treat 'em mean, keep 'em keen. Nothing seems to work. It always ends the same: alone on a park bench, crying lonely tears as happy couples pass by, hugging our bottle of cider like it was the mother we never had.

The aim of this book is not to describe the many reasons why we've been dumped. Our goal is to impart the ways we've found to move on. Consider this your first step out of the 'binge drinking, Radiohead listening, crank phone calls in the middle of the night' hole you've found yourself in.

Your feelings will change as you progress through your heartache so we've sectioned this book to reflect the various stages along the highway out of Splitsville. How quickly you move through these stages is up to you, but don't rush it. Things need to take their natural course. Follow the suggestions that best suit you and you'll soon be back to your normal degenerate self.

You'll also find personal stories of our own so you know you're not alone. If you can beat any of them in terms of sheer ridiculous cruelty, then you really are in trouble, but at least, you've got this book. We had to go it alone and make the kind of mistakes that only lawyers can benefit from.

Now, it's time to forge ahead. Be brave, little
Grasshopper.   This isn't going to be easy, but
there's a hundred and one ways out of this and we're
going to show you each and every one.

DAMAGE CONTROL
IN THE EARLY DAZE

You're single again. Despite all her promises and declarations of love, she still ducked out and left you with a broken heart and the sudden need to drink Absinthe from the bottle. How could she be so cruel? So two-faced? Anthropologists tell us we are descended from monkeys, but this is only partly true. Men evolved from monkeys. It explains our back hair and the need to scratch ourselves in public. Women, however, descended from snakes, which explains their tendency to slowly strangle the life out of their victim before casually devouring them whole. That or inject their prey with venom which, once it reaches the heart, causes an emasculating paralysis of limb and independent thought.

The hard fact of the matter is - she simply doesn't want to be with you any more. Right now, she's probably cackling her flabby arse off as she drops another newt's eye into her cauldron. She had her reasons for leaving and you have to respect that.

Strength comes from the ability to move on and to do what is necessary to get your life back on track. It has nothing to do with feeling miserable and alone. These are natural side effects to what is essentially a shit situation. Now is the time to be strong.

Forget all those questions currently buzzing around your head - Why did she leave? What did I do wrong? Why did she buy sexy underwear hours before dumping me? The only question you have to consider is - What do I do now? Because the decisions you make in the next few days could be crucial to your mental health.

Don't obsess about her next boyfriend. He has as many problems as you. If you can't help thinking about him, then imagine him as the walking STI he probably is. You're better than him and she'll soon realise it, but by then you'll be dating a Swedish bikini model. And her twin sister. If you want to be proactive, find some dirt on him and blackmail the bastard into dumping her.

It's inevitable that she'll move on. As the Dumpee, you might find it a little harder, but that doesn't mean you should envy New Bloke. What's to envy about a man whose house is about to be turned into a bomb site of facial creams and feminine hygiene products? From now on, it's his movies that are going to be interrupted with 'What's he doing now?' and 'Doesn't she look nice in that dress?' Don't feel jealous, feel pity.

Slag off her parents for no other reason than they are probably slagging you off.

Have a good old cry, but not in public. The only people who can get away with crying in public are children who've dropped their ice cream, drunken women whose breasts have dropped and mime artists. You'll be seen as the town nut job and the only sympathy you'll get is from the social worker who takes you away to a nice, safe place. And that's only because she's paid to.

Crying in the privacy of your own home is a valuable experience. Men tend to withhold their emotions rather than express them in streams of tears and snot. However unmanly it feels, it's a healing process and will put you in the right frame of mind for what is truly manly - revenge.

Rent movies with no romance and plenty of violence. Oh, and zombies. Zombies are a particularly relevant subject matter because they have something in common with your Ex. They too want to rip your heart out, only they'll probably want to eat it as well.

At this stage, the last thing you need is Hugh Grant and his rom-com buddies telling you everything will have a happy ending. Chances are, she won't come back to you in floods of tears. You won't chase her to the airport before persuading her to forget her flight to Peru. Truth is, you'll be lucky if she returns your Madness CD's.

At least, you know what you're getting with a good zombie flick - an unfeasible plot, a group of strangers thrown together in an unlikely struggle for survival and head wounds inflicted via shotgun and/or railway spike. Wouldn't you rather face a future like that than one containing Hugh Grant? Bring on the brains!

Tell all your friends about her sexual hang-ups. It will remind you she wasn't the siren you remember her as. Let's face it, she never did that thing you like. Not even on your birthday. When she was drunk. And you'd already bought the strap-on.

But tell her parents that she did.

Go to a Star Trek convention. You can wander around stalls peopled by spotty teenagers dressed as the Borg secure in the knowledge that you at least had a girlfriend.

Don't rush into another long-term relationship. Right now, you're damaged goods and women can spot that a mile off. You'll get dumped again and your Ex will find out. It will confirm she made the right decision and you'll have two Ex's to avoid at parties.

People often barge headlong into a new relationship to find a replacement for the one they just lost, but after a split, the Ex becomes an idealised version of herself. You forget she shaved her bikini line in the back yard. You forget she called premium rate lines in the desperate hope of winning a set of stainless steel pans worth half the cost of the telephone call. In your memory, she becomes perfect. How can New Girl be expected to live up to that?

In time, you'll remember your Ex as the trouble spot she really was and it will put you in a better position to forgive New Girl the first time she blows the covers off the bed.

There are certain rules in life that are inherently true; eyeballs are best left in eye sockets rather than presented as the first course in a Japanese restaurant; gravity is only beneficial when you're on the ground, not when you've just slipped off the top rung of a ladder; and men are petty, petty creatures. Revenge is a manly thing and a dish best served cold, unlike beans on toast.

The 'That-Will-Teach-Her' school of thought is a popular one because it helps vent those inner frustrations that would otherwise eat you up like a tribe of bald-headed cannibals.

Buy her a gift of friendship to show there are no hard feelings. Think along the lines of pinless grenades, a letter from the STI clinic confirming what you both knew to be true or the say-it-with-love Taliban-O-Gram.

Go to a gym. Good health makes you feel more confident and let's face it, only cows should have four stomachs. This is particularly relevant if you're so deluded you eat pizza everyday, having convinced yourself you need a daily intake of Vitamin Cheese.

The gym is also home to hordes of sweaty women pumping up and down on various machines. If you squint your eyes and the light is just right, you can pretend they are doing something naughty. Bear in mind that your membership will be revoked should you be caught sniffing the seats afterwards.

Hose yourself down and go to a lap-dancing bar. Contrary to popular belief, babes in thongs are not cheap so this will be a costly outing. However, while that nest egg of yours makes sound financial sense, it isn't going to get you boobs hanging off your ears, but it's worth the investment. It will remind you your Ex's boobs only hung off your ears when they weren't hanging over her shoulders.

There is a strict 'look, but don't touch' policy and as always, a stray finger can get you into a lot of trouble. Respect the gals as artisans of the ancient craft of naked waggle dancing and behave yourself.

Remember what your mother told you - look with your eyes, not with your tongue.

Move away from the area. It's good to get some distance between you and the girl who destroyed your faith in womankind.

Find yourself a bachelor pad and make it your own. If that bachelor pad happens to be above a brothel, then so be it.

Buy a dog and pour all your unrequited love into it. Not literally, of course. Bestiality is still illegal, even in Wales.

Dogs are affectionate, loyal creatures and therefore unlikely to remind you of your Ex. In fact, the only thing they have in common is that they are both dumber than a bag of hammers and have a tendency to leave little messages around the house (in case of your Ex, usually on notes reading - Keep Off My Yoghurts, Fat Boy).

Join the circus. It provides a great opportunity to travel the world in a rickety caravan and use Port-A-Loos on an alarmingly regular basis.

The downside is your colleagues will comprise of scary looking clowns and tightrope walkers who fell off, cracked their spine and now spend their days sweeping out elephant shit because they didn't bother to go to school.

If you had the rare type of Ex that bought you things, sell them, too. You don't need daily reminders that she once valued you enough to buy you a dancing Elvis statue or that book on how to perform decent oral sex.

Vagina is actually Latin for money grabbing Gorgon and there's no need to be out of pocket. Chances are, she's left you with nothing but credit card bills and hairy bailiffs at your door requesting you fork over your hand-crafted sex toys.

Go out with your friends. They know what's best for you...just hope it's getting so drunk you try lighting your cigarette from a running tap.

It's going to be odd calling friends you ignored while going out with her. The moment you re-introduce yourself, they'll know you're after something, but if they are true friends, they'll understand.

Your friends have always been there for you. They were there when you broke your leg in junior school and cried like a baby (in fact, they probably had something to do with it). They were there when you got your first kiss, first car, first job. They were there for the first time you had a wank in the staff canteen and got sacked. Well, not literally, we hope.

You're going to need some support and friends can offer you that, even if it's just because they know they'll get dumped one day and need to make sure you'll do the same for them.

Try to be friends with her. We know it's difficult at first, but it's amazing how little interest you take in her prattling on when you're not going to get sex out of it.

However, you must set boundaries. Listening to how New Bloke made her multi-orgasm simply by dropping his Mr. Men underpants will only make you re-consider that penis extension she suggested to you when you first started going out.

Avoid becoming her Shag Buddy. At the back of her mind, she's thinking of the guy she's scared of asking out because he's blatantly too good for her.

PERSONAL STORY

Shaun says - "I thought myself a penis genius when it came to the tactics I used to turn an Ex into a Shag Buddy. I knew from previous experience that simply blurting out the phrase - 'Fancy a fuck?' - would only ever get me in one bed; a hospital one."

"This particular Ex seemed to get hornier the more chocolate I fed her. So after one huge sugar rush, I happened to mention my lack of sex life and oh-where-oh-where would I get some luck. She fell for it and immediately began expounding the virtues of Shag Buddyism (which is much like Shag Buddhism, but with fewer nappies). It worked like a charm! I mean, here I was being asked by a beautiful woman to sleep with her on the condition it meant nothing to me. I had the keys to the Universe and it was all good."

"But of course, it wasn't, was it? As the great philosopher Heraclitus said, 'No man can cross the same river twice' or to put it more simply, you can't go back and expect everything to be the same. I thought we could return to our adventurous, just-on-the-wrong-side-of-the-law sex life and everything would be fine."

"Old feelings were sparked by our physical intimacy and while I was starting to feel emotional toward her, she just wanted to be banged."

"I began to feel like a prostitute, but without the reassurance of payment. I couldn't blame her. I thought I could keep my physical and emotional needs separate, but when you make a Shag Buddy from an Ex, this is almost impossible."

"In the end, it felt like I lost her twice."

Have a Mid-Life crisis. You might as well get all the shit times in your life over with in one go. It provides the perfect excuse to buy a Ferrari and date a masseuse twenty years your junior. Unless you're thirty.

Have a playful snowball fight with snowballs secretly containing dog shite. When she asks where you keep finding all this brown snow, simply smile, wink and hit her between the eyes. Same goes for that batch of yellow snow you cooked up earlier that day.

Be warned – hurling excreta, or to give it its technical name 'Bum Goodies' can lead to blindness. Should this unfortunate event occur, spin her around three times really fast and piss off home without her.

Send back all the love letters she wrote. If you don't, you'll read them over and over, analysing her lies in the hope of discovering what went wrong. This is about as productive as building a submarine out of soap. Unless you find 'Your cock is too small' written in secret ink, you're wasting everyone's time.

Sending them back will force her to realise she may once have been human before turning into Arachnia, Queen of the Stubbly Legged Spiders, spinning her web of deceit and trapping innocent and horny souls.

For added catharsis, try defacing the letter with 'Your tits are too small' in secret ink.

See a counsellor. If you can't unload your problems onto a guy in corduroys and knitwear, you really are in trouble. Friends can only listen to your whining for so long before the term 'friendship' becomes synonymous with the term 'anchor dragging me down into the pits of despair.' They have their own problems to deal with, like how they're going to get your Ex into bed without you knowing.

A counsellor is a trained expert in listening and understanding. So even when they can not be bothered and would rather be at home wearing their wife's knitwear, they have to sit there and pretend.

Be warned – this level of caring doesn't come cheap so make sure you make it worth your while. Don't limit yourself to problems with you Ex, chat about everything that's troubling you, like the dysfunctional relationship you have with your parents and the time the shampoo bottle got stuck on your knob.

Hang out with your divorced Dad. He's been there and knows how hard it can be. The latent hostility he harbours toward your Mother will be refocused on to your Ex. Swap stories about their irritating habits, generally cold demeanour and their unreasonable attitude toward blow-jobs.

Make a tape of uplifting songs and listen to it as often as possible. This is a reinforcement technique designed to trick you into thinking you're happy.

Suggested songs include - "My New Girl likes porn," "I can drink in my underpants if I want to (sha-la-la)," and "I did your sister while you holidayed in Crete."

Keep a diary charting the ups and downs of your life without her. It can help to put everything in perspective.

Your bible of truth will act as a defence against the rumours she's no doubt spreading about your hideous habits, like picking grapes up with your arse cheeks. Damn it, man! It's a great party trick, but not when you're doing the weekly shop.

Be prepared for her painting herself as the victim of your wanton cruelties in the same breath as she tries to justify why she ran off with a brick-layer from Peebles.

Take her out and get her drunk. This will give you an opportunity for an honest and open discussion about why she broke your heart.

More importantly, you can wait until she passes out, shave her head, glue the hair to her chin with a sign saying 'You - in fifty years time.'

Get into the habit of calling your Ex what she is - 'Bitch,' 'Two-timer,' 'Pygmy arsed banshee,' 'Bug eyed shite harvester,' 'Poisonous thorn on the flower of your existence'...need we go on?

Calling her 'The Love of your Life' will only prolong the agony.

When people ask how you're feeling, don't pretend everything is okay. Tell them what's really going on in your head. It's healthy to talk about your worries. They'll soon lose interest after the first five hours, so keep to the relevant points.

Go for long walks through beautiful scenery. Simple exercise relieves stress while the landscape distracts your attention from the love she so expertly faked.

Avoid long walks that entail you pacing up and down her street for three hours a day.

Smile. Even though it may be the last thing you want to do, smiling releases endorphins in the system by mere association. Our advice - smile at that nineteen year old female shoe shop clerk. Smile at the single mother as you give up your seat for her on the bus. Smile at the homeless woman desperate to make some money.

Avoid Thom Yorke from Radiohead like the plague. He's probably a really happy go-lucky chap. He just doesn't come across that way.

Start collecting novelty items as a hobby. It will provide you with something to concentrate on other than what she's doing with her New Bloke, but don't collect things from her rubbish bin. It's creepy.

We suggest something with a little more edge to it than porcelain hedgehogs. Star Wars figures rock (the vintage ones, of course) or why not collect the souls of the damned? It all depends on what kind of display cabinet you have.

Buy satellite TV. The endless channels of mindless crap could numb anyone. There's a lot of dross, but highlights include 'Topless Darts,' 'Presidential Mud-Wrestling' and 'Enema Your Neighbour.'

Dale Winton sometimes gets on, too.

Invest in pornography. Invest so much, in fact, that you have to build an extension to your house to store it all.

Popular titles include 'Slutty Teens and Flaming Queens,' 'Mature Like Good Cheese' and 'Hairy Mary and her Travelling Circus of Cock Clowns.'

Looking at these divine creatures in a number of compromising positions will give you an appreciation of how out of shape your Ex was. And how frigid.

If you've been kicked out the house you paid half the mortgage on, don't spend too much time on your mate's couch. Be sure you get what's yours. Love comes and goes, but money can buy that wide screen TV she wouldn't let you have.

You can't afford to give up on all the possessions you bought by working in that shitty office. Remain strong for those awkward conversations where you nit-pick over who gets the house and who gets the life size replica of Mr. T.

Discover your inner peace through spiritualism. This is a great way of easing your anxieties and restoring your chi, but don't go too far - no-one likes a hippy.

Take a vow of celibacy. This is completely different from being unable to get another girlfriend. At least, that's what we tell ourselves.

And don't forget, the single lifestyle has many benefits: sole possession of the remote control, no need to share the chocolate digestives, no requirement to wear underwear and no need to hide the fact you've been thinking about her mother's funbags while enjoying your vodka breakfast for one.

Decorate your flat/house/the bedroom in your parents' house where she wasn't allowed to stay anyway. Removing all visible traces of your Ex is one step toward removing the painful memories and it means you can finally get rid of her creepy clown doll that watches you while you sleep.

This is your chance to stamp your new identity as single Cad About Town on your environment. Buy posters of Miss January and that tennis bird with the itchy arse.

Read Paradise Lost by John Milton. It makes you look educated and by the time you actually finish the damn thing, you'll find five months have past and you can't even remember the name of the vacuous moose who dumped you in the first place.

Dress up as a woman. There's a great tradition among English men of donning a frock and parading up and down in front of full-length mirrors. We're not entirely sure how beneficial this will be to you, but wouldn't it be cool if you turned out to be better looking than your Ex?

Quit your job. Data entry and professional brown-nosing are all very well, but why deny yourself the dream of selling the Big Issue with only lice in your crusty beard for company? You've fucked up your personal life. You may as well go the whole nine yards.

Give up smoking. Of course, this only applies if you smoked in the first place. We could advocate taking up smoking then quitting immediately after, but this seems as useful as tits on a giraffe.

Smoking has gone the way of opium as a socially acceptable habit. Blowing smoke rings through your nose is only funny when fire-eaters do it and something has gone dangerously wrong. Smoking causes cancer, heart disease, impotence, bad breath and Bill Gates' jumpers. At least four of the last five are true, though all are pretty terrifying.

Giving up nicotine as your best friend may seem like a silly thing to do right now, especially as you seem to need it now more than ever, but it will provide a huge distraction from the other reason your heart isn't functioning properly.

Go on a bender. Get yourself all dressed up, break out your least troubled credit cards and hit the town - big style.

At this point, only God knows what will happen. On the one hand, you might end up winning big at the casino, be invited to a celebrity party and find yourself sandwiched between Keira Knightley and Kirsten Dunst like oh so lucky strawberry jam. Or you'll wake up four weeks later in casualty with a broken jaw you received from the WPC, who arrested you for being naked and interfering with a traffic cone.

PERSONAL STORY

Graham says - "Splitting from one girlfriend, I went on a bender for a month. I would sit in my bedroom drinking cheap vodka and watching films like 'Death Avalanche of Doomly Destruction: 2' and 'Floppy; The Crime Fighting Rabbit'."

"Not surprisingly, I don't remember much from this period of my life, other than my wake up call. Venturing from the swamp that had once been my bedroom, I found myself staggering from pub to pub one Saturday evening when I literally bumped into my Ex. She was at a hen party and wearing a tight fitting leopard skin dress with kitty ears to match (favoured by high class hookers and low class safari guides). Truthfully, she looked as great as I pictured her in every tortured dream I had had since she dumped me."

"The look that passed over her face was not one of familiarity, but one of disgust. To say I'd let myself go was an understatement. She had clearly moved on, masking any upset she might have felt under a sexy dress and the expensive perfume I'd bought her in Turkey (so what if it left a rash? She smelled nice)."

"In that one look, I knew I couldn't go on the way I was behaving. I was wearing my heart on my sleeve, together with several lager and vomit stains."

"I believe that stewing in alcohol for a month was part of a necessary process in feeling better, but every healing process must come to an end. I have since learned to deal with trauma in a more constructive manner and rarely watch films about avalanches anymore."

Go mad. There's a good chance you're a fair way down that path already. Why not listen to what your fractured mind is trying to tell you and go bat-shit crazy? Cut off all social contact, deprive yourself of sleep, listen to evil music and blow your biscuit over innocent passers-by.

Give this a couple of weeks and you'll have forgotten all about the pain she put you through. The downside is that you'll probably start to believe you're dating Margaret Thatcher as you paddle your bath around the pond of your local park wearing nothing, but a huge, false beard.

Get cryogenically frozen. This is the ultimate moving on technique. Let the years fly by as icicles form on your bollocks. When you wake centuries later, be sure to stop by the cemetery and dance on her grave.

The problem is that those grey-faced boffins have yet to cure the freezing process and you may end up dying. We're sure they'll crack this in the next millennium, but by that time they'll probably have cured heartache as well, making the whole thing fucking redundant.

Perform a goodbye ritual. This is a symbolic gesture aimed at forcing you to move on, but avoid anything that involves goat's blood.

Items required: any photos or letters from her, bottles and bottles of alcohol, a free evening, the next day free for recovery and a nice little treat for after. May we suggest eating fromage frais from a lap-dancer's cleavage?

The ritual is complicated, but also a whole lot of dangerous fun. Get very nude, swig frequently from your drink of choice and gyrate hypnotically to a nice banjo solo. Call on a higher force to release the pain from within. Might be a good idea to call the Samaritans, too.

CAN'T LET G●

The initial shock is over, but the emptiness remains. It's perfectly understandable that you would want her back. Think about all the good times you had together. All the laughs and wild, shameful sex.

Think positive. It's also possible to get her back and the second time around could be better than the first. You both know what went wrong so fixing those problems should be a cinch.

We'll support you no matter what, but we offer a word of caution. Love is very much like the Star Wars movies. It starts off as a wonderful journey, full of excitement, passion and the Millennium Falcon. You have a break, but there's a light at the end of the galaxy. Lo and behold, here comes the chance to start afresh. A new episode begins, but you can tell it's not the same. It feels more like hard work than fun. Cracks begin to appear and the relationship takes a nose-dive into all too familiar territory. She tells you she was briefly seeing a guy from Accounts called Jar Jar Binks and you know the whole thing was doomed from the start.

It's your choice, but the best time to strike is before the dust has had chance to settle and she's feeling confused and alone. She'll still be missing you and therefore more likely to forgive your many misdemeanours.

Women can be fickle creatures prone to mood swings that will leave you more muddled than a puppy with two pricks. Jump in now while the pendulum swings in your favour.

May the Force be with you.

Create a voodoo doll in her likeness. The possibilities at this point are limited only by your imagination, but we would like to offer a few suggestions.

You could use it to convince her that your habit of choosing which underwear based on the scratch-and-sniff method is entirely loveable. Furthermore, trimming your corns at her parent's dinner table and your predilection for lighting your farts to brown the Shepherd's Pie are also acceptable.

Plant demoralising statements into her subconscious by saying things like - "When a woman's looks begin to fade, it all boils down to cooking skills," "Cases of STI's are on the rise and men are more likely to lie about having them" and "So, are you still passing the pencil test?" Without her knowing, you'll have whittled her confidence down to nothing and she'll be ready to take you back.

This is an underhanded trick and only works if you don't get caught. If nabbed, she'll realise what a weasel you truly are and it's game over, man. Game over.

Remember, women are a lot like fog - they mask on-coming trouble and, at times, are quite dense. If you can subtly convince her she's not the bloke magnet she believes she is, you can step in as the hero charitably taking on the scraps no-one else wants.

God bless you and your big heart.

Pretend to be friends while trying to win her back. This is a dangerous option, but appealing to the desperate. Remember all the reasons she dumped you and turn them around - "Oh, yes," you say. "I love children and your mother is an absolute delight to be around."

The danger is she may accept your offer of friendship, but spurn your advances. This leaves you in the unenviable position where you still have to go shopping with her, but without the possibility of a blow-job as a reward.

Her close proximity is sure to tug on your heart strings while her emotional distance is likely to take those heart strings and choke you with them.

Get plastic surgery. Being ugly is only okay if you want to study science. Of course she said she didn't mind your lazy eye/six-fingered hands/six-fingered chest, but what she was really saying was - "I'm glad you've got a car." In fact, when you told her about the growth on your neck, she'd assumed you meant your head.

Going under the knife isn't about bar room fights any more. For a reasonable fee, you can have your body parts stretched into impossible and beautiful shapes, but as ever - let caution be your guide. No-one wants to be known as Fishlips Magoo.

Become her shag buddy. If you're old enough to have sex, you're old enough to know begging for it comes with the territory.

It's an excellent way of getting rid of your pent up frustrations whilst providing much needed exercise.

Impress her with the benefits of having done twenty tongue push-up's every morning and make her head spin. Remember the age old proverb - If a woman leaves walking like John Wayne, she is sure to return.

Sympathise with her when she worries about her looks. It will show her the sensitive side you kept buried so long under your many neuroses and bouts of binge drinking.

You should have been doing this all along. Women like to believe they are attractive, even when it is blatantly untrue and she has more wrinkles than Yoda's scrotum.

Except you didn't do any of that, did you, dipshit? Otherwise, you wouldn't be single and have taken to wearing your tear-stained Thundercats pyjamas all day long.

You know what her fears are so exploit them with kind words and convincing lies.

Convince her that men with small knobs are the best shags. Please. If one of them starts to believe it, they all will.

Get her locked away in a mental institution. It shouldn't be difficult to persuade a psychiatrist that any woman is madder than a box of monkeys. You can then be sure that she'll never meet anyone again. As long as it's a hospital staffed by ugly, non-sexual doctors.

Again - not too difficult.

Try to emulate someone you respect and admire. Taking on their qualities will help you re-build your confidence, shaping you into the man you used to be, but don't go so far as to dress like them. If you start dressing like Rod Stewart, you'll lose her forever.

This is a standard practice in most confidence building seminars. If you're sick of looking at your pale, tired face in the mirror, choose to see a young Al Pacino instead. Imagine, how he'd react to getting his Ex back. There'd be a trademark Hoo-Hah, a devilish, shit eating grin and the absolute certainty in his bloodshot eyes that his Ex will be taking off her bra in under ten seconds flat.

PERSONAL STORY

Graham says - "Watching the behaviour and mannerisms of Clooney and Pitt in Ocean's Eleven made me realise what a loser I had become. Everything about them was as sleek as a greased otter. I sat watching these kings of charisma in my Spiderman underwear eating chicken in a basket knowing something had to be done."

"It would take more than robbing a casino to make me cool. It would take nice suits, great hair and some witty repartee."

"So I pushed the boat out. More than £5 for a haircut, more than £20 for a suit. Combined, even I had to admit I was looking razor fine, but those guys had more than just looks. They had what the French call - coconuts of steel and those I couldn't get from Oxfam."

"Yet the strangest thing happened. When I donned the clobber and styled the hair, I suddenly felt like I was ready to steal a million and win the girl in the process. I was a colossus striding through the bars of my home town. My confidence was back and this time, it was personal."

"I knew it would be only a matter of time before I bumped into my Ex. I felt sure she'd freeze on the spot from the mere coolness of my presence. At that point, I'd throw a Pall Mall in my mouth, raise a sardonic eyebrow and wait for the broad to fall for the con."

Read women's magazines. We're talking about magazines written by women as opposed to magazines featuring women, spread-eagled and riding a feathered dildo.

There was a time when these rags were nothing more than a collection of knitting patterns and make-ups tips. They were bought by the kind of woman who used so much hairspray the only brand they could truly trust was cement.

Those days are gone. For some reason, women now want to know more than how to cook the perfect plum pudding. The articles provide a fascinating insight into the minds of women, thus giving you an advantage over your competition. They feature do's and don'ts for men and how to win a harlot's heart.

If that's not enough, there are heart warming stories to cheer you up, like how a bride got stood up at the altar while the groom knobbed one of the fat bridesmaids in the vestry.

Go to a beauty parlour to sexify yourself. It's increasingly common for men to get wrapped in seaweed while some seventeen year old bubble head grinds away their corns. But remember to come up with a decent excuse as to why you're there because the minute you step outside, all your mates will be passing by. With your Dad, confirming what he long suspected since catching you putting on your Mother's make-up aged seven.

PERSONAL STORY

Shaun says - "Like most men, I am secretly insecure about my looks. Excuses like "It's a fuel tank for a sex machine" or "It's a solar panel for a pervert" only got me so far and getting dumped confirmed my worst held suspicions."

"But beauty parlours are expensive places. It costs a high percentage of your meagre wages and an awful lot of dignity when you see the withering looks from under the heavily made up eyes of the therapists. My solution was to go to a college where students are more than happy to see a walking guinea pig to practise on."

"I felt oddly at ease as I walked into the room. The girls looked professional. They wore white coats and everything. It wasn't until later I remembered butchers wore the exact same outfit, but with slightly less foundation and more pig's blood."

"I thought I'd start off slow - a nice massage and maybe a facial. I reasoned hard arse waxing could wait until my self-hatred built to an extreme level. But I'd failed to specify this when I made my appointment and the therapists were calling the shots."

"Today's lesson was the removal of red veins in the face by electrolysis. Ironically, years of heavy drinking had provided my face with enough burst veins to look like a road map of Luton. The game was on."

"I lay down on the bed while a crowd of twittering therapists surrounded me. The lecturer wheeled out a machine that looked like it had been abandoned by Dr. Frankenstein as being unsafe."

"The details of how this contraption worked escaped me, but I gathered they were about to use a needle to zap small currents of electricity into my face. The only reason I didn't cry was I knew that water and electricity don't mix."

"The next half hour passed in a blur as the therapists took turns to electrocute me. It wasn't painful as such. It was more of a slight stinging sensation as if someone had just put a jellyfish on my face and I was too polite to remove it."

"Afterwards, I was thanked for my time and asked if I wanted to return to continue the treatment. As I looked in the mirror, I saw my face was completely red and I was going to spend the rest of my life looking like I was permanently embarrassed. I declined their kind offer and explained I was washing my hair - with the trainee hairdressers down the hall."

"Of course, the redness did go away and the amount of red veins in my face was significantly reduced. If I'd been more of a man, I would have returned, but that little bit of a man that I am is an abject coward and that part always gets the ruling vote."

Get to know the kids in your area. Now listen very carefully, we mean this in the best possible way. Showing your Ex how good you are with the little shits may make her re-evaluate how lousy she thought you'd be as a Dad. Refrain from beating them for whinging on the way kids do.

Take up a martial art. It will get you ridiculously fit and means you'll look really cool while giving New Bloke a good shoeing.

We've seen the movies and we all know the path to enlightenment involves cleansing the mind and body, waxing on, waxing off and beating the shit out of complete strangers.

You may still be harbouring aggressive feelings so why not karate chop them out?

Remind her of all the good times you had. Jog her memory about the time you took her for a romantic meal and ordered champagne. Omit the fact that you didn't have the money to pay for it.

When it comes to Splitsville, the pattern is for the Dumper to focus on the negative side of the relationship and the Dumpee to focus on the positive things he just lost. You need to remind her of all the heart-warming gestures you made, like holding back her hair as she puked into her shoes or the time you didn't go ballistic when your Dad found a dirty thong down the back of the sofa, not even after you saw the pain in his eyes as he washed his hands.

Make her jealous with another woman. Laugh hysterically as you pass your Ex at the bar, arm in arm with wonderful New Girl. If you have to pay wonderful New Girl to be with you, ask for extras. No point wasting her.

PERSONAL STORY

Graham says - "I was lucky enough to be set up on a blind date weeks after a split from an Ex. I had spoken to this New Girl on a few previous occasions. She was pretty and I took the fact that she had yet to slap me as a promising beginning. However, this was something she was sure to rectify when she realised I was taking her to a party my Ex was also attending."

"We arrived fashionably late, not because we were fashionable, but because we'd missed the bus. The party was in full swing and I saw my Ex immediately. More importantly, I saw she was alone."

"New Girl and I settled down for a drink and awkward small talk. We discussed her hobbies and interests while I made up whole sections of my life in a desperate attempt to keep the conversation going. I felt it was only a matter of time before I could introduce her to my Ex in a powerful and vengeful sting operation."

"A shadow fell over us. Without looking up, I knew I had been pre-empted. My Ex was going to introduce herself and force feed me platitudes about how she was happy I'd found a new life. As I turned to face her, I found I was staring up into the face of a man. A handsome man. New Girl's Ex."

"He was sorry to interrupt and asked if he could have a quiet word with my date. Needless-to-say that was the last I saw of her, left as I was with nothing, but my overly active imagination offering me details on what they might be doing in the car park later that night."

"Ironically, my Ex had seen every minute of this mini soap opera and stopped by to offer her condolences. We had a good talk and my night was brightened when she admitted to small twinges of jealously. It wasn't much, but given the regret I could have gone home with, it was enough."

Speak to her parents. This does not mean shouting obscenities through their letterbox. Get them on your side and persuade them to put a little parental pressure on her to take you back.

This won't work, however, if you were dumped for shouting obscenities at her parents through their letterbox.

Throw a swingers' party on the same night she's dropping off your stuff. After all, she always said she wanted to share your interests.

Write a song for her and serenade her under her bedroom window, but not at three in the morning, pissed out your scalp with your pants around your ankles.

Writing a tune for her is an incredibly romantic gesture and not one often done, largely due to the bone crushing embarrassment involved. However, it does require a little musical ability. No fair maiden was ever wooed with a didgeridoo.

It also offers you the chance to express all your feelings of pain and loss. Writing down your emotions will help you understand how you really feel about her and setting them to a rumba beat is musical gold.

Act pathetic whenever she's around. The name of the game is to wheedle your way back into her affections like the ringworm you are. Doe eyes and trembling lips are the tools of your trade. Tears and a malnourished frame are your weapons of mass destruction.

This is the last gambit of the damned so be sure you're willing to go to the edge of reason for this one. If not - keep it to yourself, cry baby.

When all else fails, build a life size replica to replace her. You'll need a refrigerator motor to prevent the ice in her heart from melting and two tree trunks for legs. To make an exact duplicate, make sure she seems alive in every other room except the bedroom. Install a computer for her brain (not a very fast one, obviously) and train her to recognise simple voice commands, like - "Be quiet! The telly's on" and "Bend over and blow your nose."

PUTTING RADIOHEAD
BEHIND YOU
(THE BEGINNING
OF THE END)

You probably thought you'd never reach this stage. Your shattered personality is knitting back together nicely and those lingering feelings for her have been replaced by simple regret. It's like completing a marathon - you've got to the finishing line, but now you have to limp home and tend to your blistering sores and chaffed crotch.

Having gone through such a traumatic experience, it's likely you'll have some baggage. Not the designer Posh and Becks type of baggage, but the no self-confidence, crying in your sleep kind. It would be great if we could finish with someone and simply move on to the next Ex, but it isn't like that. Not only do women leave you, but they take your sense of worth too, along with your collection of obscene African art. Ex's aren't just for Christmas, they're for life. Especially, if you murder them.

We have to build you up. You're not out the woods yet, but it's time to take a little pleasure in your recovery. Value these days ahead and appreciate how far you've come. Get back on your donkey, Don Quixote. We're going for a ride!

Start flirting with the women in your office, even the ugly ones. It will do your confidence the world of good to realise you are still appealing to women. Plus it adds a little spice to your soul-destroying job when there's the possibility of getting a blowjob from the boss. Even if she does have a moustache to rival Freddie Mercury's.

Offices are a breeding ground for flirtatious e-mails and breast-ogling by the water cooler. It is a well known fact that many people meet their life time partners at work so it's time you cleaned yourself up. This means no more turning up hungover in last night's pants. Especially if they aren't yours. And he wants them back.

Become obsessed with a celebrity. This is the safest way to conduct your next love affair as long as you stop short of stalking. Be sure to resist the urge to steal underwear from her washing line.

This may seem a little extreme, but that's just because it is — extreme times call for extreme measures. An unattainable star is the perfect vessel for your unrequited love. How can she reject you if she doesn't know you? But remember, that's exactly the point - she should not know you and neither should her lawyer.

The trick is to take a healthy interest in her career and build an admiration from afar. There are few legitimate reasons for building a shrine.

Visit karaoke bars. For some unknown reason, they attract women in record numbers and they're generally fun loving, good time gals. Avoid the one who spent four and a half hours dressing like Cher, because chances are, 'she' is a plumber called Cowboy Dave.

Join a dating agency. These agencies specialise in bringing together people who have been betrayed by their lovers and can't be bothered to go through the rigmarole of meeting new people. Those agencies that double as massage parlours offer a different, but equally valuable service.

Do some charity work. Aiding those less fortunate than you can help you find a new appreciation of yourself as 'Man of the People.' In truth, it doesn't matter if you care about raising money for the Lesser-spotted Belgian Octopus, just so long as you know a single woman who does.

Learn a foreign language. You may be a Nobel prize winning scientist, but nothing looks more accomplished than being able to speak more than one language.

It's a great way to win over a girl on a first date. Even if you can only manage to whisper in her ear — "I fall asleep on roundabouts," you'll still be on to a winner. Tell her it was something classy about her eyes.

Pay special attention to your hygiene. We all know you don't have to wash your cock everyday, but a quick rub down never did anyone any harm. There's nothing worse than blundering your way into a surprise shag to remember you forgot to wipe your arse again that morning. Imagine the look on New Girl's face when she pulls down your trousers before being enveloped in a lime green mist. Then, imagine her walking out of the room texting her friends about the hobo she almost shagged.

Do remember to wash your bedsheets, too. No woman wants to have to tenderise the duvet before she can get in.

Visit chatrooms on the Internet. They reek of desperation, but we suspect that's just where you're at. You can brush up on your 'chatting up' skills without embarrassing yourself in front of someone you may meet the day after.

People who visit chatrooms have a ropey reputation. Not because they are mad, bad and dangerous to know, but because they are skinny, pale geeks who log on with names like — Woman4Horse and FecalJohn from Kent.

But think about it. Chatroom jockeys are often there because they do not have the opportunity to make new friends. They may be jolly, but lonely lighthouse keepers. Or a woman too fat to get out of her front door. Or a prison inmate doing a ten-to-fifteen year stretch. Whatever their circumstances, do they not deserve love, too? Probably not.

PERSONAL STORY

Shaun says — "Confession time: My name is Shaun and I visit chatrooms. One day, while bored and looking for available females, I got chatting to a guy calling himself Daddy Bear. Perhaps it was my naiveté, but I envisioned the scenario to be two men at the bar, chatting while they waited to be served before going their separate ways in search of women creatures. I was very wrong."

"Without so much as a -'Get your coat, you've pulled!' - Daddy Bear informed me he was naked, except for a pair of his mother-in-law's underwear, which he was wearing on his head. I was too shocked to respond, but remember thinking - this mulch shuffler is married and I'm the one who's single? Mr. Bear then said he had to leave because he wanted to spend the next hour or so sniffing her shoes before she got back from the shops."

"And then he was gone. My whirlwind romance over as quickly as it had began. Thank fuck for that!"

Eat chocolate. Women have known this for centuries, but indulging in large quantities of cocoa products releases the same feelings as being in love.

The irony is that eating chocolate everyday will rot your teeth and make you fatter than a fat hippo's fat arse, then no-one will love you anyway. God giveth and God taketh away.

Learn sign language. Finally, you'll have something to do with your hands that won't turn you blind.

Signing, like any other language, can be a difficult thing to learn. If practising out in the open, be careful you don't direct traffic into the sea.

Win the lottery. Although, legend holds it's not true, women do go for men with cash. And a large cock. Find the winning ticket and buy something you could use to beat a camel to death.

Enlist in the Armed Forces. There's nothing like a big, red-faced man screaming at you to do push-ups to take your mind off things emotional. So will spending years in a prisoner of war camp eating soap, but no system is perfect.

The military will teach you valuable skills in the world of espionage, torture and destroying innocent people. So, once your contract is up, you'll have more in common with women than ever before. Couple this with wartime stories of how you got injured running to the front of the dinner queue for seconds and success with the opposite sex is guaranteed.

PERSONAL STORY

Graham says - "Bizarrely enough, a soon to be Ex agreed to marry me if I joined the Navy. When I think back at how fucked up this was, I'm amazed to remember I got as far as the recruitment office."

"A kindly old man, who looked like he'd never shouted at a new recruit in his life, sat me down and told me all about the wonderful opportunities to be had in the Navy, like drowning or being eaten by sharks."

"In truth, it did sound like an exciting and worthwhile career, but I began to think about my motivations behind enlisting. Why would a woman want to marry me when there was every chance I could be away from home six months out of every year? And while away, there was a real chance I could be killed? It didn't add up."

"I told my Ex about the recruitment office and my decision to go with a career where death was a marginal factor. We rowed. I apologised. She dumped."

Become a porn star. There are a few prerequisites to the job - twelve inches and a handle bar moustache, but the perks are second to none. Check your Mother isn't an avid viewer of porn because going round for Sunday lunch could get really awkward.

We probably won't have to push you too hard to take this option, but we're unsure how to get you started. There's no such thing as a skin-flick union and try telling a recruitment agency that, instead of wasting your precious time in a soul-destroying in a soul-destroying call centre, you would rather spend your days being licked like a lollipop by Asian triplets.

Happy is the man whose work is also his hobby.

Go to University. They say a good education is the cornerstone of a successful future. This is bollocks, of course, but as a soap-dodging student, you will get discounts everywhere from the video store to your local STI clinic.

Get domesticated. Just as cavemen spent centuries trying to civilise dogs and horses, women have been trying to do the same with men. If women really like the rough and ready type, why do they insist on us using knives and forks? As ever, women claim one thing but want another.

Stop burying your turds in the sand-pit and learn how to knock up a decent lasagne.

Read 'The Naked Ape' by Desmond Morris. This insightful book is full of interesting information on the human condition. The chapter on 'Sex' ought to be every man's Bible. Plus it answers that question which plagues us all after a day-long drinking session - why do men have nipples?

Memorise a romantic poem. Reciting a line or two of poetry to a possible conquest is a great seduction technique. Choose an obscure poem she won't know and claim you wrote it. Avoid limericks that start with "There was a girl called Big Gash."

Drink alone in a bar. In American films, drinking alone means you'll be guaranteed to be approached by good looking femmes fatales. In England, it means you're a candidate for Alcoholics Anonymous and likely to sell your Grandmother's leg for the next vodka coke. In any case, it indicates you're available. Possibly too available.

Get religion. Believing in something that could be a complete hoax seems like a waste of time. The majority of churchgoers are old people hedging their bets. However, it's free bread and wine on Sundays and you stand a chance of being forgiven for sneaking a peek at your best mate's girlfriend's biff.

Being religious gives you an inner strength often lacking in today's society and getting in with a guy who can change water into wine can't be bad, either.

P.S. Graham and Shaun respect the right of individuals to follow any religious beliefs they want. They also ask you to put in a word for them if you die before they do.

Go on a reality TV show. For most of you, death would be a more preferable option, but you might get a few rounds of buff the muff in the shower. Plenty of careers have then been built by opening supermarkets and appearing in piss-poor pantomimes.

Become a male escort. You'll get paid for going out with rich, sexually frustrated older women, though it's not a great career to tell your Gran about. Especially, if she wants in on the action.

Consider it a master class in charm with the added advantage of being paid extra for pulling your pants down. If James Bond wasn't a killer of three-nippled Scaramanga types, then he'd be a male whore. He wouldn't be running around in a tuxedo, either. It would be quick release pants fashioned by Q. Isn't that something to aspire to?

Make a pact with Satan. Well, if the God thing doesn't work out, there's only one other guy who can help - the red, scary one. A minor word of caution - although selling your soul will buy you as many birds as your tiny bits can handle, it does tend to mean an eternity of damnation so check the contract for get out clauses. Red hot pokers up the bot is not all it's cracked up to be. Plus, as Satan is the epitome of all evil, he's probably going to be a woman so watch out.

Memorise jokes from stand up comedians. Women love a guy who can laugh them into bed. It happens a lot to us, but for different reasons. You'll never be stuck for something to say if you can whip out the one about the nun with syphilis.

Go somewhere to meet the right kind of woman. Pubs and clubs are all very well, but the sweet, loveable birds you want to meet are probably in the library borrowing books on self-confidence. The added advantage is you'll probably not be shit-faced and sporting urine stains down the front of your chinos. We said probably.

Get a blow-up doll. When the problems of a meaningful relationship can be reduced to punctures and friction burns, you must be on to a good thing. Just make sure she doesn't cheat on you with your dinghy.

Problems only arise when you start taking your doll to parties as your date. You will be assaulted with an array of questions, all somehow focusing on the fragile state of your mental health. If she starts answering those questions for you, followed by phrases like - "Kill them all," it's time to be single again.

Find out what went wrong with your last relationship. Writing the whole thing off as the Ice Queen's fault blinds you to the chance of improving your luck next time.

Make no mistake, it's going to be painful as a paper cut to your jap's eye. No-one wants to be told they're demanding, possessive or flaccid and your natural reaction will be to defend that time she caught you pissing in the sink and splashing her toothbrush.

Nobody really understands what a woman wants from a man, except that it's generally unattainable and has something to do with celebrating your anniversary with more than a chilli kebab.

Your Ex will have formed a well-founded opinion on what's wrong with you. In fact, she's probably prepared a hundred page dossier on the subject just in case you were interested, so ask her.

Rather than be defensive, why not try to take some of her thoughts on board? Those idiosyncrasies you thought were excusable quirks will no doubt be revealed as excusable as blowing bubbles up a dog's arse.

Ask coupled friends to set you up. We know they are smug, self-satisfied drones more interested in tossing salads with Jamie Oliver than getting a life, but single women seem to flock to them like skinheads to a rally.

Couples know the intimate details of everyone's life as they thrive on gossip they aren't interesting enough to generate themselves. They'll tip you off the minute a girl gets dumped and you can steam on in there with condolences and a cheeky condom in your pocket.

Get a sex change. This is a little drastic, but if you can't beat them, and you're tired of beating yourself, join them. The upside is you'll have your own set of breasts and you may get closer to understanding the perplexing, arcane and often malevolent world of women. On the downside, they chop your cock off. Your call.

Form a cult. Becoming the mysterious leader of a new cult means you can make the rules up as you go (so much like being a woman, then.) You can pave your way for ascension to Pluto by sleeping with your trusting disciples, wearing nothing, but hemp sandals.

Religions get tax benefits and you never know, you could be right.

Talk to all those girls you fancied while going out with her. Unfortunately, you'll probably find they're not half as attractive as they were when misplaced guilt prevented you from doing anything with them in the first place.

If you're lucky, you might be able to wring some pity out of them and pity has got plenty of people laid.

Go speed dating. This is a fun new way of meeting people as desperate as you. It's quick and simple - much like your bedroom technique.

The premise is very similar to making a presentation to your boss. You haven't got a clue what you're talking about, but you hope the fact that you're wearing a new shirt will make up for it.

The greatest advantage is the amount of women you will meet. Ask any Lothario and they'll tell you dating is a numbers game. The more women you talk to, the more chance you'll have of going home with her number and a tingly feeling in your special place.

Throw a 'The Bitch Dumped Me' party. This is a great way to advertise your availability. You'll find there are women out there you didn't even know about just waiting to have a crack at you. Decorate your house with pictures of your Ex at her worst. Make sure there's laminated copies taped to the toilet bowl so your guests can piss on her the way she pissed on you.

Fun party games include 'Castrate the Monk,' 'Hide and Suck' and the more traditional 'Postman's Cock.'

Become a footballer/singer/actor etc. Women the world over will adore you. This is because they are stupid.

Write a book on all the different ways you've tried to get the heartless harpy out of your mind.

**YOUR SHIT
DON'T STINK**

Congratulations mate! You made it! You are now a fully-fledged member of the brotherhood. As our favourite German once said - "What doesn't kill me makes me stronger." Having gone through all that, we figure you're strong enough to bench press an elephant's arse and still have the muscle power to compete against all those unfortunate souls who are still to have their heart broken.

There are benefits to being cast down into the gutter and crawling your way back up to the light. You now know how resilient you can be in the face of female adversity. Unlike others, you know the havoc women can cause and know you can overcome it as bravely and as confidently as the man who faces oncoming traffic with clean underwear.

Despite it all, women make our world turn. We've called her the type of names you have to use a dictionary to figure out, but your Ex only did what she thought best and contrary to all scientific data, women are human, too.

You may be asking yourself - so what now? Well, your options are limitless. You could decamp to the Amazon rainforest, lick toads and live a life of psychedelic serenity. Or write an opera about streetwise orphans and their struggle to legalise pick pocketing. Or invent a zip that doesn't come undone when you're asking your boss for a raise/sexy rub down/quick transfer to another office to save further embarrassment. Whatever you choose, your future should be brighter in the light of your new-found knowledge.

Remember the lessons you've learnt. You can't protect yourself against heartache. Love, like the baton of the riot police, can come crashing down on you irrespective of what you happen to be doing at the time. You made it through once. You can do it again.